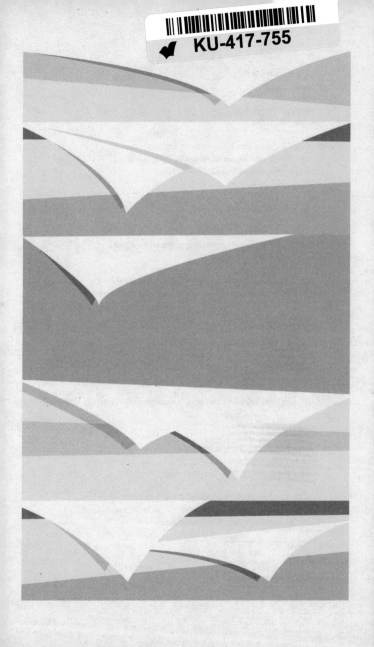

1 3 5 7 9 10 8 6 4 2

Vintage
20 Vauxhall Bridge Road,
London SW1V 2SA

Vintage Classics is part of the Penguin Random House
group of companies whose addresses can be found at
global.penguinrandomhouse.com

Penguin
Random House
UK

Extract from *Something Happened* copyright © Scapegoat
Productions, Inc. 1996, 1974

Joseph Heller has asserted his right to be identified as the author of this
Work in accordance with the Copyright, Designs and Patents Act 1988

First published in Great Britain in 1974 by Jonathan Cape
First published by Vintage in 1995
A portion of this book first appeared in *Esquire*
This short edition published by Vintage in 2017

penguin.co.uk/vintage

A CIP catalogue record for this book is available from the British Library

ISBN 9781784872786

Typeset in 9.5/14.5 pt FreightText Pro
by Jouve (UK), Milton Keynes
Printed and bound by Clays Ltd, St Ives plc

Penguin Random House is committed to a sustainable future for
our business, our readers and our planet. This book is made from
Forest Stewardship Council® certified paper.

MIX
Paper from
responsible sources
FSC® C018179
FSC
www.fsc.org

Work

JOSEPH HELLER

VINTAGE MINIS

The office in which I work

IN THE OFFICE in which I work there are five people of whom I am afraid. Each of these five people is afraid of four people (excluding overlaps), for a total of twenty, and each of these twenty people is afraid of six people, making a total of one hundred and twenty people who are feared by at least one person. Each of these one hundred and twenty people is afraid of the other one hundred and nineteen, and all of these one hundred and forty-five people are afraid of the twelve men at the top who helped found and build the company and now own and direct it.

All these twelve men are elderly now and drained by time and success of energy and ambition. Many have spent their whole lives here. They seem friendly, slow, and content when I come upon them in the halls (they seem dead) and are always courteous and mute when they ride with others in the public elevators. They no longer work hard. They hold meetings, make promotions, and allow their names to be used on announcements that are prepared and issued by somebody else. Nobody is sure anymore who really runs the company (not even the people who are credited with running it), but the company does run. Sometimes these twelve men at the top work for the government for a little while. They don't seem interested in doing much more. Two of them know what I do and recognize me, because I have helped them in the past, and they have been kind enough to remember me, although not, I'm sure, by name. They inevitably smile when they see me and say: 'How are you?' (I inevitably nod and respond: 'Fine.') Since I have little contact with these twelve men at the top and see them seldom, I am not really afraid of them. But most of the people I am afraid of in the company are.

Just about everybody in the company is afraid of somebody else in the company, and I sometimes think I am a cowering boy back in the automobile casualty insurance company for which I used to work very long ago, sorting and filing automobile accident reports after Mrs Yerger was placed in charge of the file room and kept threatening daily to fire us all. She was a positive, large woman of overbearing confidence and nasty amiability who never doubted the wisdom of her biases. A witty older girl named Virginia sat under a big Western Union clock in that office and traded dirty jokes with me ('My name's Virginia—Virgin for short, but not for long, ha, ha.'); she was peppy and direct, always laughing and teasing (with me, anyway), and I was too young and dumb then to see that she wasn't just joking. (Good God—she used to ask me to get a room for us somewhere, and I didn't even know how! She was extremely pretty, I think now, although I'm not sure I thought so then, but I did like her, and she got me hot. Her father had killed himself a few years before.) Much went on there in that company too that I didn't know about. (Virginia herself had told me that one of the married claims adjusters had taken her out in his car one night, turned insistent, and threatened to rape her or put her out near a cemetery, until she pretended to start to cry.) I was afraid to open doors in that company too, I remember, even when I had been sent for by one of the lawyers or adjusters to bring in an important file or a sandwich. I was never sure whether to knock or walk right in, to tap deferentially or rap loudly enough to be heard at once and command admission. Either way, I would often encounter expressions of annoyance and impatience (or feel I did. I had arrived too soon or arrived too late).

Mrs Yerger bullied us all. In a little while, nearly all of the file clerks quit, a few of the older ones to go into the army or navy, the rest of us for better jobs. I left for a job that turned out to be worse. It took nerve to give notice I was quitting, and it always has. (I rehearsed my resignation speech for days, building up the courage to deliver it, and formulated earnest, self-righteous answers to accusing questions about my reasons for leaving that neither Mrs Yerger nor anyone else even bothered to ask.) I have this thing about authority, about walking right up to it and looking it squarely in the eye, about speaking right out to it bravely and defiantly, even when I know I am right and safe. (I can never make myself believe I *am* safe.) I just don't trust it.

That was my first job after graduating (or being graduated *from*) high school. I was seventeen then—that 'older,' witty, flirting girl under the Western Union clock, Virginia, was only twenty-one (too young now by at least a year or two, even for me)—and in every job I've had since, I've always been afraid I was about to be fired. Actually, I have never been fired from a job; instead, I receive generous raises and rapid promotions, because I am usually very alert (at the beginning) and grasp things quickly. But this feeling of failure, this depressing sense of imminent catastrophe and public shame, persists even here, where I do good work steadily and try to make no enemies. It's just that I find it impossible to know exactly what is going on behind the closed doors of all the offices on all the floors occupied by all the people in this and all the other companies in the whole world who might say or do something, intentionally or circumstantially, that could bring me to ruin. I even torture myself at times with the ominous speculation that the CIA, FBI, or Internal Revenue Service has been investigating me surreptitiously for years and is about to close in and arrest me, for no other reason than that I have some secret liberal sympathies and usually vote Democratic.

I have a feeling that someone nearby is soon going to find out something about me that will mean the end, although I can't imagine what that something is.

———

IN THE NORMAL course of a business day, I fear Green and Green fears me. I am afraid of Jack Green because my department is part of his department and Jack Green is my boss; Green is afraid of me because most of the work in my department is done for the Sales Department, which is more important than his department, and I am much closer to Andy Kagle and the other people in the Sales Department than he is.

Green distrusts me fitfully. He makes it clear to me every now and then that he wishes to see everything coming out of my department before it is shown to other departments. I know he does not really mean this: he is too busy with his own work to pay that much attention to all of mine, and I will bypass him on most of our assignments rather than take up his time and delay their delivery to people who have (or think they have) an immediate need for them. Most of the work we do in my department is, in the long run, trivial. But Green always grows alarmed when someone from another department praises something that has come from my department. He turns scarlet with rage and embarrassment if he has not seen or heard of it. (He is no less splenetic if he *has* seen it and fails to remember it.)

The men in the Sales Department like me (or pretend to). They don't like Green. He knows this. They complain about him to me and make uncomplimentary remarks, and he knows this too. He pretends he doesn't. He feigns indifference, since he doesn't really like the men in the Sales

Department. I don't really like them, either (but I pretend I do). Generally, Green makes no effort to get along with the men in the Sales Department and is pointedly aloof and disdainful. He worries, though, about the enmity he creates there. Green worries painfully that someday soon the Corporate-Operations Department will take my department away from his department and give it to the Sales Department. Green has been worrying about this for eighteen years.

IN MY DEPARTMENT, there are six people who are afraid of me, and one small secretary who is afraid of all of us. I have one other person working for me who is not afraid of anyone, not even me, and I would fire him quickly, but I'm afraid of him.

THE THOUGHT OCCURS to me often that there must be mail clerks, office boys and girls, stock boys, messengers, and assistants of all kinds and ages who are afraid of *everyone* in the company; and there is one typist in our department who is going crazy slowly and has all of *us* afraid of *her*.

Her name is Martha. Our biggest fear is that she will go crazy on a weekday between nine and five. We hope she'll go crazy on a weekend, when we aren't with her. We should get her out of the company now, while there is still time. But we won't. Somebody should fire her; nobody will. Even Green, who actually enjoys firing people, recoils from the responsibility of making the move that might bring about her shattering collapse, although he cannot stand her, detests the way she looks, and is infuriated by every reminder that she still exists in his department. (It was he who hired her after a cursory interview, on the strong recommendation of the woman in the Personnel Department who is in charge of finding typists and sending them up.) Like the rest of us, he tries to pretend she isn't there.

We watch her and wait, and pussyfoot past, and wonder to ourselves how much more time must elapse before she comes on schedule to that last, decisive second in which she finally does go insane—shrieking or numb, clawing wildly or serene, comprehending intelligently that she has now gone mad and must therefore be taken away, or terrified, ignorant, and confused.

Oddly, she is much happier at her job than the rest of us. Her mind wanders from her work to more satisfying places, and she smiles and whispers contentedly to herself as she gazes out over her typewriter roller at the blank wall only a foot or two in front of her face, forgetting what or where she is and the page she is supposed to be copying. We walk away from her if we can, or turn our backs and try not to notice. We each hope somebody else will do or say something to make her stop smiling and chatting to herself each time she starts. When we cannot, in all decency, delay any longer doing it ourselves, we bring her back to our office and her work with gentle reminders that contain no implication of criticism or reproach. We feel she would be surprised and distraught if she knew what she was doing and that she was probably going mad. Other times she is unbearably nervous, unbearable to watch and be with. Everyone is very careful with her and very considerate. Green has complained about her often to the head of Personnel, who does not want to fire her either and has contacted her family in Iowa. Her mother has married again and doesn't want her back. Martha has bad skin. Everyone resents her and wishes she would go away.

THE COMPANY IS benevolent. The people, for the most part, are nice, and the atmosphere, for the most part, is convivial. The decor of the offices, particularly in the reception rooms and anterooms, is bright and colorful. There is lots of orange and lots of sea green. There are lots of office parties. We get all legal holidays off and take days off with pay whenever we need them. We have many three- and four-day weekends. (I can't face these long weekends anymore and don't know how I survive them. I may have to take up skiing.)

Every two weeks we are paid with machine-processed checks manufactured out of stiff paper (they are not thick enough to be called cardboard) that are patterned precisely with neat, rectangular holes and words of formal, official warning in small, black, block letters that the checks must not be spindled, torn, defaced, stapled, or mutilated in any other way. (They must only be cashed.) If not for these words, it would never occur to me to do anything else with my check but deposit it. Now, though, I am occasionally intrigued. What would happen, I speculate gloomily every two weeks or so as I tear open the blank, buff pay envelope and stare dully at the holes and numbers and words on my punched-card paycheck as though hoping disappointedly for some large, unrectifiable mistake in my favor, if I did spindle, fold, tear, deface, staple, and mutilate it? (It's my paycheck, isn't it? Or is it?) What would happen if, deliberately, calmly, with malice aforethought and obvious premeditation, I disobeyed?

I know what would happen: nothing. Nothing would happen. And the knowledge depresses me. Some girl downstairs I never saw before (probably with a bad skin also) would simply touch a few keys on some kind of steel key punch that would set things right again, and it would be as though I had not disobeyed at all. My act of rebellion would be absorbed like rain on an ocean and leave no trace. I would not cause a ripple.

I suppose it is just about impossible for someone like me to rebel anymore and produce any kind of lasting effect. I have lost the power to upset things that I had as a child; I can no longer change my environment or even disturb it seriously. They would simply fire and forget me as soon as I tried. They would file me away. That's what will happen to Martha the typist when she finally goes crazy. She'll be fired and forgotten. She'll be filed away. She'll be given sick pay, vacation pay, and severance pay. She'll be given money from the pension fund and money from

I suppose it is just about impossible for someone like me to rebel anymore

the profit-sharing fund, and then all traces of her will be hidden safely out of sight inside some old green cabinet for dead records in another room on another floor or in a dusty warehouse somewhere that nobody visits more than once or twice a year and few people in the company even know exists; not unlike the old green cabinets of dead records in all those accident folders in the storage room on the floor below the main offices of the automobile casualty insurance company for which I used to work when I was just a kid. When she goes crazy, her case will be closed.

I had never imagined so many dead records as I saw in that storage room (and there were thousands and thousands of even deader records at the warehouse I had to go to once or twice a year when a question arose concerning a record that had been dead a really long time). I remember them accurately, I remember the garish look of the data in grotesquely blue ink on the outside of each folder: a number, a name, an address, a date, and an abbreviated indication of whether the accident involved damage to property only (PD) or damage to people (PI, for personal injury). Often, I would bring sandwiches from home (baloney, cooked chopped meat with lots of ketchup, or tuna fish or canned salmon and tomato) and eat them in the storage room downstairs on my lunch hour, and if I ate there alone, I would read the New York *Mirror* (a newspaper now also dead) and then try to entertain myself by going through some old accident folders picked from the file cabinets at random. I was searching for action, tragedy, the high drama of detective work and courtroom suspense, but it was no use. They were dead. None of the names or appraisals or medical statements or investigations or eyewitness reports brought anything back to life. (The *Mirror* was better, and even its up-to-the-minute true stories of family and national misfortunes read just like the comic strips.) What impressed me most was the sheer immensity of all those dead records, the abounding quantity of all those drab old sagging cardboard file cabinets rising like joined, ageless towers from the floor almost to the ceiling, that vast, unending sequence of unconnected accidents that had been happening to people and cars long before I came to work there, were happening then, and are happening still.

There was a girl in that company too who went crazy while I was there. She was filed away. And in the company I worked for before this one, there was a man, a middle-minor executive, who went crazy and jumped out of a hotel window and killed himself; he left a note saying he was sorry he was jumping out of the hotel window and killing himself, that he would have shot himself instead but didn't know how to obtain a gun or use one. He was picked up off the ground by the police (probably) and filed away.

I think that maybe in every company today there is always at least one person who is going crazy slowly.

THE COMPANY IS having another banner year. It continues to grow, and in many respects we are the leader in the field.

According to our latest Annual Report, it is bigger and better this year than it was last year.

We have twenty-nine offices now, twelve in this country, two in Canada, four in Latin America, and eleven overseas. We used to have one in Cuba, but that was lost. We average three suicides a year: two men, usually on the middle-executive level, kill themselves every twelve months, almost always by gunshot, and one girl, usually unmarried, separated, or divorced, who generally does the job with sleeping pills. Salaries are high, vacations are long.

People in the company like to live well and are unusually susceptible to nervous breakdowns. They have good tastes and enjoy high standards of living. We are well-educated and far above average in abilities and intelligence. Everybody spends. Nobody saves. Nervous breakdowns are more difficult to keep track of than suicides because they are harder to recognize and easier to hush up. (A suicide, after all, is a suicide: there's something final about it. It's the last thing a person does. But who knows with certainty when a person is breaking down?) But nervous breakdowns do occur regularly in all age and occupational groups and among all kinds of people—thin people and fat people, tall people and short people, good people and bad people. In the few years I have been in charge of my department, one girl and one man here have each been out for extended absences because they broke down. Both have been fixed and are now back working for me, and not many people outside my department know why they were gone. (One of them, the man, hasn't been fixed too well, I think, and will probably break down again soon. He is already turning into a problem again, with me and with everyone else he talks to. He talks too much.)

In an average year, four people I know about in the company will die of natural causes and two-and-a-half more (two men one year, three the next) will go on sick leave for ailments that will eventually turn out to be cancer. Approximately two people will be killed in accidents every year, one in an auto, the other by fire or drowning. Nobody in the company has yet been killed in an airplane crash, and this is highly mysterious to me, for we travel a lot by air to visit other offices or call on customers, prospects, and suppliers in other cities and countries. When regular, full-time employees do go on sick leave, they are usually paid their full salary for as long as the illness lasts (even though it may last a lifetime. Ha, ha), for the company excels in this matter of employee benefits. Everybody is divorced (not me, though). Everyone drinks and takes two hours or more for lunch. The men all flirt. The women all respond, except for a few who are very religious or very dull, or a few very young ones who are out in the world for the first time and don't understand yet how things are.

Most of us like working here, even though we are afraid, and do not long to leave for jobs with other companies. We make money and have fun. We read books and go to plays. And somehow the time passes.

———

THIS FISCAL PERIOD, I am flirting with Jane. Jane is new in the Art Department and not quite sure whether I mean it or not. She is just a few years out of college, where she majored in fine arts, and still finds things in the city daring, sophisticated, and intellectual. She goes to the movies a lot. She has not, I think, slept with a married man yet.

Jane is assistant head of the Art Department in Green's department. There are only three people in the Art Department. She has, like the rest of us, much time in which to brood and fantasize and make personal phone calls and kid around with whoever in the company (me) wants to kid around with her. She has a tall, slim figure that's pretty good and a clogged duct in one eye that makes it dribble with tears. She wears loose lamb's-wool sweaters that hug the long points of her small breasts beautifully. (Often, my fingertips would love to hug and roll those same long points of her small breasts just as beautifully, but I know from practice that my desire would not remain with her breasts for long. They make a convenient starting place.) Her good figure, prominent nipples, and clogged tear duct give me easy openings for suggestive wisecracks that cover the same ground as those I used to exchange with that older girl Virginia under that big Western Union clock in the automobile casualty insurance company (the company is still in business after all these years, at the same place, and probably the clock too is still there, running, although the office building is now slated to come down), except that now I am the older, more experienced (and more jaded) one and can control and direct things pretty much the way I choose. I have the feeling now that I can do whatever I want to with Jane, especially on days when she's had two vodka martinis for lunch instead of one (I, personally, hate vodka martinis and mistrust the mettle of people who drink them) or three whiskey sours instead of two. I could, if I wished, take her out for *three* vodka martinis after work one day and then up to Red Parker's apartment nearby, and the rest, I'd bet, would be as easy as pie (and possibly no more thrilling). I can make Jane laugh whenever I want to, and this, I know, can be worth more than half the game if I ever decide I seriously do want to play, but *I'm* not sure either whether I mean it or not.

Probably, I should be ashamed of myself, because she's only a decent young girl of twenty-four. Possibly I should be proud of myself, because she is, after all, a decent and very attractive young girl of only twenty-four whom I can probably lay whenever I want to. (I have her scheduled vaguely somewhere ahead, probably in the weeks before the convention, when I will be using everybody in the Art Department a great deal.) I don't really know how I am supposed to feel. I do know that girls in their early twenties are easy and sweet. (Girls in their late twenties are easier but sad, and that isn't so sweet.) They are easy, I think, because they are sweet, and they are sweet, I think, because they are dumb.

On days when *I've* had two martinis for lunch, Jane's breasts and legs can drive me almost wild as she parks her slender ass against the wall of one of the narrow corridors in the back offices near the Art Department when I stop to kid with her. Jane smiles a lot and is very innocent (she thinks I'm a very nice man, for example), although she is not, of course, without some sex experience, about which she boasts laughingly when I taunt her with being a virgin and denies laughingly when I taunt her with being a whore. I make teasing, rather mechanical and juvenile jokes (I've made them all before to other girls and ladies in one variation or another) about her eye or sweater or the good or bad life I pretend she is leading as I lean down almost slavering toward the front of her skirt (I don't know how she can bear me in these disgusting moments—but she can) and gaze lecherously over the long stretch of her thighs underneath, even though I know already I would probably find her legs a little thin when I had her undressed and would probably describe her as a bit too skinny if I ever spoke about her afterward to anyone.

I think I really do like Jane a lot. She is cheerful, open, trusting, optimistic—and I don't meet many of *those* anymore. Till now, I've decided to do nothing with her except continue the lascivious banter between us that tickles and amuses and encourages us both. Maybe her face and her figure are a little too good. I used to like girls who were tall and heavy, and slightly coarse, and maybe I still do, but I seem to be doing most of my sleeping these days with girls who are slim and pretty and mostly young. My wife is tall and slim and used to be very pretty when she was young.

———

THE PEOPLE IN the company who are most afraid of most people are the salesmen. They live and work under pressure that is extraordinary. (I would not be able to stand it.) When things are bad, they are worse for the salesmen; when things are good, they are not much better.

They are always on trial, always on the verge of failure, collectively and individually. They strain, even the most secure and self-assured of them, to look good on paper; and there is much paper for them to look good on. Each week, for example, a record of the sales results of the preceding week for each sales office and for the Sales Department as a whole for each division of the company is kept and compared to the sales results for the corresponding week of the year before; the figures are photocopied on the latest photocopying machines and distributed throughout the company to all the people and departments whose work is related to selling. In addition to this, the sales record for each sales office for each quarter of each year for each division of the company and for the company as a whole is tabulated and compared to the sales record for the corresponding quarter of the year before; along with this, cumulative quarterly sales totals are also kept, and all these quarterly sales totals are photocopied and distributed too. In addition to this, quarterly and cumulative sales totals are compared with quarterly and cumulative sales totals* (*estimated) of other companies in the same field, and these figures are photocopied and distributed too. The figures are tabulated in stacks and layers of parallel lines and columns for snap comparisons and judgments by anyone whose eyes fall upon them. The result of all this photocopying and distributing is that there is almost continuous public scrutiny and discussion throughout the company of how well or poorly the salesmen in each sales office of each division of the company are doing at any given time.

When salesmen are doing well, there is pressure upon them to begin doing better, for fear they may start doing worse. When they are doing poorly, they are doing terribly. When a salesman lands a large order or brings in an important new account, his elation is brief, for there is danger he might lose that large order or important new account to a salesman from a competing company (or from a competing division of this company, which shows how complex and orderly the company has become) the next time around. It might even be canceled before it is filled, in which case no one is certain if anything was gained or lost. So there is crisis and alarm even in their triumphs.

Nevertheless, the salesmen love their work and would not choose any other kind. They are a vigorous, fun-loving bunch when they are not suffering abdominal cramps or brooding miserably about the future; on the other hand, they often turn cranky without warning and complain and bicker a lot. Some sulk, some bully; some bully and then sulk. All of them drink heavily until they get hepatitis or heart attacks or are warned away from heavy drinking for some other reason, and all of them, sooner or later, begin to feel they are being picked on and blamed unfairly. Each of them can name at least one superior in the company who he feels has a grudge against him and is determined to wreck his career.

The salesmen work hard and earn big salaries, with large personal expense accounts that they squander generously on other people in and out of the company, including me. They own good houses in good communities and play good games of golf on good private golf courses. The company encourages this. The company, in fact, will pay for their country club membership and all charges they incur there, if the club they get into is a good one. The company seeks and rewards salesmen who make a good impression on the golf course.

Unmarried men are not wanted in the Sales Department, not even widowers, for the company has learned from experience that it is difficult and dangerous for unmarried salesmen to mix socially with prominent executives and their wives or participate with them in responsible civic affairs. (Too many of the wives of these prominent and very successful men are no more satisfied with their marital situation than are their husbands.) If a salesman's wife dies and he is not ready to remarry, he is usually moved into an administrative position after several months of mourning. Bachelors are never hired for the sales force, and salesmen who get divorced, or whose wives die, know they had better remarry or begin looking ahead toward a different job.

(Red Parker has been a widower too long and is getting into trouble for that and for his excessive drinking. He is having too good a time.)

Strangely enough, the salesmen, who are aggressive, ego-tistical, and individualistic by nature, react very well to the constant pressure and rigid supervision to which they are subjected. They are stimulated and motivated by discipline and direction. They thrive on explicit guidance toward clear objectives. (This may be one reason golf appeals to them.) For the most part, they are cheerful, confident, and gregarious when they are not irritable, anxious, and depressed. There must be something in the makeup of a man that enables him not only to *be* a salesman, but to *want* to be one. Ours actually *enjoy* selling, although there seem to be many among them who suffer from colitis, hernia, hemorrhoids, and chronic diarrhea (I have one hemorrhoid, and that one comes and goes as it pleases and is no bother to me at all, now that I've been to a doctor and made sure it isn't cancer), not to mention the frequent breakdowns from tension and overwork that occur in the Sales Department as well as in other departments, and the occasional suicide that pops up among the salesmen about once every two years.

The salesmen are proud of their position and of the status and importance they enjoy within the company, for the function of my department, and of most other departments, is to help the salesmen sell. The company exists to sell. That's the reason we were hired, and the reason we are paid.

———

THE PEOPLE IN the company who are least afraid are the few in our small Market Research Department, who believe in nothing and are concerned with collecting, organizing, interpreting, and reorganizing statistical information about the public, the market, the country, and the world. For one thing, their salaries are small, and they know they will not have much trouble finding jobs paying just as little in other companies if they lose their jobs here. Their budget, too, is small, for they are no longer permitted to undertake large projects.

Most of the information we use now is obtained free from trade associations, the U.S. Census Bureau, the Department of Commerce, the U.S. Chamber of Commerce, the National Association of Manufacturers, and the Pentagon, and there is no way of knowing anymore whether the information on which we base our own information for distribution is true or false. But that doesn't seem to matter; all that does matter is that the information comes from a reputable source. People in the Market Research Department are never held to blame for conditions they discover outside the company that place us at a competitive disadvantage. What is, is—and they are not expected to change reality but merely to find it if they can and suggest ingenious ways of disguising it. To a great extent, that is the nature of my own work, and all of us under Green work closely with the Sales Department and the Public Relations Department in converting whole truths into half truths and half truths into whole ones.

I am very good with these techniques of deception, although I am not always able anymore to deceive myself (if I were, I would not know that, would I? Ha, ha). In fact, I am continually astonished by people in the company who do fall victim to their own (our own) propaganda. There are so many now who actually believe that what we do is really important. This happens not only to salesmen, who repeat their various sales pitches aloud so often that they acquire the logic and authority of a mumbo-jumbo creed, but to the shrewd, capable executives in top management, who have access to all data and ought to know better. It happens to people on my own level and lower. It happens to just about everybody in the company who graduated from a good business school with honors: these are uniformly the most competent and conscientious people in the company, and also the most gullible and naïve. Every time we launch a new advertising campaign, for example, people inside the company are the first ones to be taken in by it. Every time we introduce a new product, or an old product with a different cover, color, and name that we present as new, people inside the company are the first to rush to buy it—even when it's no good.

When salesmen and company spokesmen begin believing their own arguments, the result is not always bad, for they develop an outlook of loyalty, zeal, and conviction that is often remarkably persuasive in itself. It produces that kind of dedication and fanaticism that makes good citizens and good employees. When it happens to a person in my own department, however, the result can be disastrous, for he begins relying too heavily on what he now thinks is the truth and loses his talent for devising good lies. He is no longer convincing. It's exactly what happened to Holloway, the man in my own department who broke down (and is probably going to break down again soon).

'But it's true, don't you see?' he would argue softly to the salesmen, the secretaries, and even to me, with a knowing and indulgent smile, as though what he was saying ought to have been as obvious to everyone as it was to him. 'We *are* the best.' (The point he missed is that it didn't matter whether it was true or not; what mattered was what people *thought* was true.)

He is beginning to smile and argue that way again and to spend more time talking to us than we want to spend listening to him. My own wish when he is buttonholing me or bending the ear of someone else in my department is that he would hurry up and have his nervous breakdown already, if he is going to have one anyway, and get it—and himself—out of the way. He is the only one who talks to Martha, our typist who is going crazy, and she is the only one who listens to him without restlessness and irritation. She listens to him with great intensity because she is paying no attention to him at all.

Everyone grew impatient with him. And he lost his power to understand (as he is losing this power again) why the salesmen, who would come to him for solid proof to support their exaggerations and misrepresentations, turned skeptical, began to avoid him, and refused to depend on him any longer or even take him to lunch. He actually expected them to get by with only the 'truth.'

It's a wise person, I guess, who knows he's dumb, and an honest person who knows he's a liar. And it's a dumb person, I guess, who's convinced he is wise, I conclude to myself (wisely), as we wise grown-ups here at the company go gliding in and out all day long, scaring each other at our desks and cubicles and water coolers and trying to evade the people who frighten us. We come to work, have lunch, and go home. We goose-step in and goose-step out, change our partners and wander all about, sashay around for a pat on the head, and promenade home till we all drop dead. Really, I ask myself every now and then, depending on how well or poorly things are going with Green at the office or at home with my wife, or with my retarded son, or with my other son, or my daughter, or the colored maid, or the nurse for my retarded son, is this *all* there is for me to do? Is this really the *most* I can get from the few years left in this one life of mine?

And the answer I get, of course, is always . . . *Yes!*

Because I have my job, draw my pay, get my laughs, and seem to be able to get one girl or another to go to bed with me just about every time I want; because I am envied and looked up to by neighbors and coworkers with smaller salaries, less personality, drab wives; and because I really do seem to have everything I want, although I often wish I were working for someone other than Green, who likes me

We goose-step in and goose-step out, change our partners and wander all about, sashay around for a pat on the head, and promenade home till we all drop dead and likes my work but wouldn't let me make a speech at the company convention in Puerto Rico last year, or at the company convention in Florida the year before—and who knows I hate him for that and will probably never forgive him or ever forget it.

(I have dreams, unpleasant dreams, that relate, I think, to my wanting to speak at a company convention, and they are always dreams that involve bitter frustration and humiliation and insurmountable difficulty in getting from one location to another.)

GREEN NOW THINKS I am conspiring to undermine him. He is wrong. For one thing, I don't have the initiative; for another, I don't have the nerve; and for still another thing, I guess I really like and admire Green in many respects (even though I also hate and resent him in many others), and I know I am probably safer working for him than I would be working for anyone else—even for Andy Kagle in the Sales Department if they did decide to move me and my department from Green's department to Kagle's department.

In many ways and on many occasions Green and I are friends and allies and do helpful, sometimes considerate things for each other. Often, I protect and defend him when he is late or forgetful with work of his own, and I frequently give him credit for good work from my department that he does not deserve. But I never tell him I do this; and I never let him know when I hear anything favorable about him.

I enjoy seeing Green apprehensive. I'm pleased he distrusts me (it does wonders for my self-esteem), and I do no more than necessary to reassure him.

And I am the best friend he has here.

So I SCARE Green, and Green scares White, and White scares Black, and Black scares Brown and Green, and Brown scares me and Green and Andy Kagle, and all of this is absolutely true, because Horace White really is afraid of conversation with Jack Green, and Johnny Brown, who bulldozes everyone around him with his strong shoulders, practical mind, and tough, outspoken mouth, is afraid of Lester Black, who protects him.

I know it's true, because I worked this whole color wheel out one dull, wet afternoon on one of those organizational charts I am always constructing when I grow bored with my work. I am currently occupied (as one of my private projects) with trying to organize a self-sufficient community out of people in the company whose names are the same as occupations, tools, or natural resources, for we have many Millers, Bakers, Taylors, Carpenters, Fields, Farmers, Hammers, Nichols (puns are permitted in my Utopia, else how could we get by?), and Butchers listed in the internal telephone directory; possibly we'd be a much better organization if all of us were doing the kind of work our names suggest, although I'm not sure where I'd fit in snugly there, either, because my name means nothing that I know of and I don't know where it came from.

Digging out valuable information of no importance distracts and amuses me. There are eleven Greens in the company (counting Greenes), eight Whites, four Browns, and four Blacks. There is one Slocum . . . me. For a while, there were two Slocums; there was a Mary Slocum in our Chicago office, a short, sexy piece just out of secretarial school with a wiggling ass and a nice big bust, but she quit to get married and was soon pregnant and disappeared. Here and there in the company colored men, Negroes, in immaculate white or blue shirts and very firmly knotted ties are starting to appear; none are important yet, and nobody knows positively why they have come here or what they really want. All of us (almost all of us) are ostentatiously polite to them and pretend to see no difference. In private, the salesmen make jokes about them.

('Know what they said about the first Negro astronaut?'
'What?'
'The jig is up.')

I am bored with my work very often now. Everything routine that comes in I pass along to somebody else. This makes my boredom worse. It's a real problem to decide whether it's more boring to do something boring than to pass along everything boring that comes in to somebody else and then have nothing to do at all.

Actually, I enjoy my work when the assignments are large and urgent and somewhat frightening and will come to the attention of many people. I get scared, and am unable to sleep at night, but I usually perform at my best under this stimulating kind of pressure and enjoy my job the most. I handle all of these important projects myself, and I rejoice with tremendous pride and vanity in the compliments I receive when I do them well (as I always do). But between such peaks of challenge and elation there is monotony and despair. (And I find, too, that once I've succeeded in impressing somebody, I'm not much excited about impressing that same person again; there is a large, emotional letdown after I survive each crisis, a kind of empty, tragic disappointment, and last year's threat, opportunity, and inspiration are often this year's inescapable tedium. I frequently feel I'm being taken advantage of merely because I'm asked to do the work I'm paid to do.)

On days when I'm especially melancholy, I begin constructing tables of organization from standpoints of plain malevolence, dividing, subdividing, and classifying people in the company on the basis of envy, hope, fear, ambition, frustration, rivalry, hatred, or disappointment. I call these charts my Happiness Charts. These exercises in malice never fail to boost my spirits—but only for a while. I rank pretty high when the company is analyzed this way, because I'm not envious or disappointed, and I have no expectations. At the very top, of course, are those people, mostly young and without dependents, to whom the company is not yet an institution of any sacred merit (or even an institution especially worth preserving) but still only a place to work, and who regard their present association with it as something temporary. To them, it's all just a job, from president to porter, and pretty much the same job at that. I put these people at the top because if you asked any one of them if he would choose to spend the rest of his life working for the company, he would give you a resounding *No!*, regardless of what inducements were offered. I was that high once. If you asked me that same question today, I would also give you a resounding *No!* and add:

'I think I'd rather die now.'

But I am making no plans to leave.

I have the feeling now that there is no place left for me to go.

NEAR THE VERY bottom of my Happiness Charts I put those people who are striving so hard to get to the top. I am better off (or think I am) than they because, first, I have no enemies or rivals (that I know of) and am almost convinced I can hold my job here for as long as I want to and, second, because there is no other job in the company I want that I can realistically hope to get. I wouldn't want Green's job; I couldn't handle it if I had it and would be afraid to take it if it were offered. There is too much to do. I'm glad it won't be (I'm sure it won't be).

I am one of those many people, therefore, most of whom are much older than I, who are without ambition already and have no hope, although I do want to continue receiving my raise in salary each year, and a good cash bonus at Christmastime, and I do want very much to be allowed to take my place on the rostrum at the next company convention in Puerto Rico (if it will be Puerto Rico again this year), along with the rest of the managers in Green's department and make my three-minute report to the company of the work we have done in my department and the projects we are planning for the year ahead.

It was downright humiliating to be the only one of Green's managers left out. The omission was conspicuous, the rebuff intentionally public, and for the following four days, while others had a great, robust time golfing and boozing it up, I was the object of expressions of pity and solemn, perfunctory commiseration from many people I hate and wanted to hit or scream at. It was jealousy and pure, petty spite that made Green decide abruptly to push me off the schedule after we were already in Puerto Rico and the convention had gotten off to such a promising start, and after I had worked so long and nervously (I even rehearsed at home just about every night—to the wonder and consternation of my family) on my speech for the three-minute segment of the program allotted to me and had prepared a very good and witty demonstration of eighteen color slides.

'Stop sulking,' Green commanded me curtly, wearing that smile of breezy and complacent innocence he likes to affect when he knows he is cutting deep. 'You're a rotten speaker anyway, and you'll probably be much happier working the slide machines and movie projectors and seeing that the slides of the others don't get all mixed up.'

'I want to do it, Jack,' I told him, trying to keep my voice strong and steady. (What I really wanted to do was burst into tears, and I was afraid I would.) 'I've never made a speech at a convention before.'

'And you aren't going to make one now.'

'This is a good talk I've got here.'

'It's dull and self-conscious and of no interest to anyone.'

'I've prepared some fine slides.'

'You aren't going to use them,' he told me.

'You did the same thing to me in Florida last year.'

'And I may do it again to you next year.'

'It isn't fair.'

'It probably isn't.'

I waited. He added nothing. He is so much better at this sort of ego-baiting than I am. It was my turn to speak, and he had left me nothing to say.

'Well,' I offered, shrugging and looking away.

'I don't care if it's fair or not,' he continued then. 'We're discussing an important company convention, not a college commencement exercise. I've got to use what little time they give us on the program as effectively as possible.'

'It's only three minutes,' I begged.

'I can use those three minutes better than you can.' He laughed suddenly, in the friendliest, most inoffensive fashion, as though nothing of consequence had just happened, letting me know in that arrogantly firm and rude manner of his that the argument was over. 'You must understand,

Bob,' he bantered (while I thought he might actually throw an arm around my shoulder. He never touches me), 'that this ambition of yours to make a little speech is nothing more than a shallow, middle-class vanity. I'm as shallow as you are, and as middle class as the best of them. So I'm going to take your three minutes away from you and cover you and your department in my own speech.'

You bastard, I thought. 'You're the boss,' I said.

'That's right,' he retorted coldly. 'I am. And you've already received more than enough attention here for an employee of mine. I want to make certain that nobody in this company gets the idea you're working for Andy Kagle and not for me. Or that you're doing a better job in your position than I'm doing in mine. Do you get what I mean?'

I certainly did, then. Green was reasserting his ownership of me publicly by demonstrating his right to treat me with contempt. And in his own long (rather self-conscious and pedantic) speech to the convention, he 'covered' me and my department in a single aside:

'And Bob Slocum and his people will help, when you feel you really need them, provided your requests are not unreasonable.'

And that was all, even though the two projects I had prepared for the coming year were the real high spots of the whole convention. Everyone was enthusiastic about them, even executives from other divisions of the company, who were there as guests and observers: several asked to meet me and expressed the wish for work of similar kind and quality in their own areas of the company. I could have had a grand, triumphant time that week if not for Green (Green's?) kicking me off the schedule. The salesmen, who would have to use these projects in connection with their own work, congratulated me over and over again and never stopped slapping my back as they drank their whiskey in the evening and their Bloody Marys at breakfast in the morning (although some were already implying that they would want to discuss some modifications with me for their own purposes when the convention was over and we were back in New York). And even Arthur Baron, who is boss of us all in this division, drifted over to me on the terrace of the hotel during one of the twilight cocktail parties to tell me that both my projects were the best of their kind he had ever seen and would probably be very useful.

Arthur Baron, who is tactful and soft-spoken, addressed his comments to Green, who was standing beside me on the terrace because he does not like to be seen standing alone. (I was Green's roosting place for the moment, while he took his bearings; and I knew he would walk from me to someone more important as soon as he spied an opportunity. At crowded social or business gatherings, Green never leaves one person unless he has someone else to move to.) Green laughed quickly and gave all credit for the work to me; then he promptly diminished its importance by declaring he had not even seen any of it until that same afternoon (which was not true, since his criticism and suggestions all through the previous ten weeks had helped enormously, and nothing had been included without his inspection and approval). Green went on to observe, with another pleasant laugh, that the excellent response to something prepared by me without his knowledge or assistance all went to prove what a superb administrator he was. (All I was able to get in to Arthur Baron was a mumbled:

'Thanks. I'm glad.')

'The only legitimate goal of a good administrator,' Green continued affably, smiling directly at Arthur Baron and excluding me from his attention entirely, 'is to make himself superfluous as quickly as possible, and then have no work of his own to do until he's promoted to vice-president or retires. Don't you agree?'

Arthur Baron chuckled softly in reply and said nothing. He turned from Green to me, squeezed my shoulder, and moved away. Green beamed hopefully after him, then turned somber and began to worry (I guessed) that his hint to Arthur Baron about a vice-presidency had been too broad. He was already regretting it. Green knows he often pushes too hard—even at the exact moment he is pushing too hard—but he simply cannot control himself. (He is out of his own control.)

(I am in it.) I am dependent on Green. It was Green who hired and promoted me and Green who recommends me for the generous raises and good cash bonuses I receive each year.

'You were a third-rate assistant when you came to work for me,' he likes to joke when we are getting along comfortably with each other, 'and I turned you into a third-rate manager.'

I am grateful to Green for promoting me, even though he makes fun of me often and hurts my feelings.

GREEN IS A clever tactician with long experience at office politics. He is a talented, articulate, intelligent man of fifty-six and has been with the company more than thirty years. He was a young man when he came here; he will soon be old. He has longed from the beginning to become a vice-president and now knows that he will never succeed.

He continues to yearn, and he continues to strive and scheme, sometimes cunningly, other times desperately, abjectly, ineptly, because he can neither admit nor deny to himself for very long that he has already failed. Green fawns compulsively and labors clumsily to curry favor in every contact he has with someone in top management or someone near top management. He knows he does this and is ashamed and remorseful afterward for having demeaned himself in vain; he is willing to demean himself, but not in vain. Often, he will turn perverse afterward and deliberately offend somebody important in order to restore what dignity and self-respect he feels he has lost as a man. He is a baby.

Green is a clever tactician at office politics whose major mistake has always been to overestimate the value of office politics in getting ahead. He has refused to recognize that promotion to high place in the company has invariably been based on certain abilities and accomplishments. He has never really understood why so many people of less intelligence, taste, knowledge, and imagination have gone so much further than he has and *have* become vice-presidents. He does not see that they work hard continuously and that they believe in the company, that they do well and meticulously whatever they are asked to do, that they do *everything* they are asked to do, and that they do *only* what they are asked to do—and that this is what the company wants. Green will not grant that these people are all luminously well-qualified for the higher positions into which they are moved.

At least they *appear* to be well-qualified for their new positions at the time the promotions are made. Periodically, errors occur: forecasts miscarry and people fail; a man tires, weakens in will, or buckles under new responsibilities at the office or new problems at home and ceases to operate as anticipated, and we have another minor malfunction in Personnel. We have another nervous breakdown or another executive (the envy of rivals and subordinates) who resigns (in quiet disgrace) for a job with another company or is pushed aside to allow someone else to move through or retires early or puts a bullet through his head. Periodically, I would imagine, we have single instances of all: a man breaks down, is pushed aside, resigns or retires, and then puts a bullet through his head, although I am unable to think of anyone offhand who has succeeded in traversing this full gamut of defeat. The company survives all mishaps.

While other men in high position work hard and believe in the company, Green worries hard and still tries to believe in himself. He has a vacillating infatuation for Mildred, a young, divorced girl in his department who helps coordinate production, and he surprises her often in the office, or at the banks of elevators, by kissing her suddenly and noisily on the mouth, always though with a flippant, loud remark to denote indifference and only, I suspect, when someone else is there to see. Other times he will stride past her without notice or make some terse criticism of her work or the appearance of her desk, humbling and wounding her cruelly without provocation. And she, of course, adores him in return and is scared stiff. That is, I think, the way Green wants all people to feel about him, adoring and scared stiff.

He is, I think, as big a coward as I am; yet, he is the only person in the company with enough courage to behave badly. I envy that: I am cordial and considerate to many people I detest (I am cordial and considerate to just about *everybody*, I think, except former girl friends and the members of my family); I trade jokes convivially with several salesmen who annoy the hell out of me and make me waste much of my time with their frantic and contradictory requests; I get drunk with others who bore and irritate me and join them at orgiastic parties with secretaries, waitresses, salesgirls, housewives, nurses, models from Oklahoma, and airline stewardesses from Pennsylvania and Texas; I have two men in my department I'd like to fire and one girl, and there are days when I would truly like to be rid of them all; but I try not to show how I feel, and I'll probably never do anything about any of them, except keep hoping sullenly that they'll disappear on their own; I'm glad that Martha, our crazy typist, isn't going crazy in my department, because I know that I wouldn't have the nerve or competence to do anything about her before she finally falls apart; there's a fellow executive in the Merchandising Department I have lunch with once or twice a month who I sincerely wish would drop dead. (Once a year we have him to dinner, always with a lot of other people, and once each spring he has us to lunch on his God-damned boat.) I know so many people I want to be mean to, but I just don't have the character.

Green, on the other hand, is notorious for being frank and unkind (he is frank, I suspect, *just* to be unkind). He would rather make a bad impression than no impression. He tries extremely hard to be inconsiderate to people on his own level and lower. He creates tension, terror, and uneasiness in an organization that values harmony, dreads disagreements, conceals failure, and disguises conflict and personal dislike. He is aggressive and defensive. He attacks others and is sorry for himself.

People in the company, for example, do their best to minimize friction (we are encouraged to revolve around

each other eight hours a day like self-lubricating ball bearings, careful not to jar or scrape) and to avoid quarreling
with each other openly. It is considered much better form
to wage our battles sneakily behind each other's back than to
confront each other directly with any semblance of com-
plaint. (The secret attack can be denied, lied about, or
reduced in significance, but the open dispute is witnessed
and has to be dealt with by somebody who finds the whole
situation deplorable.) We are all on a congenial, first-name
basis, especially with people we loathe (the more we loathe
them, the more congenial we try to be), and our wives and
children are always inquired about familiarly by their first
names, even by people who have never met them or met
them only once. The right to this pose of comfortable intim-
acy does not extend downward to secretaries, typists, or
mail boys, or more than two levels upward through the
executive hierarchy. I can call Jack Green Jack and Andy
Kagle Andy and even Arthur Baron Art, but I would not call
anyone higher than Arthur Baron anything but mister. That
would be not only dangerous but rude, and I am always
hesitant about being rude (to anyone but the members of
my family) even when it isn't dangerous. Even Jane in the
Art Department still calls me Mr Slocum respectfully when
we meet (sometimes by telephone appointment when I am
feeling especially frivolous) and kid around in one of the
back corridors, and Jane and I have gone pretty far with
each other by now in conversation. I used to encourage the
girls I was after to call me by my first name, but I've learned

from experience that it's always better, and safer, and more effective, to preserve the distinction between executive and subordinate, employer and employee, even in bed. (*Especially* in bed.)

People in the company are almost never fired; if they grow inadequate or obsolete ahead of schedule, they are encouraged to retire early or are eased aside into hollow, insignificant, newly created positions with fake functions and no authority, where they are sheepish and unhappy for as long as they remain; nearly always, they must occupy a small and less convenient office, sometimes one with another person already in it; or, if they are still young, they are simply encouraged directly (though with courtesy) to find better jobs with other companies and then resign. Even the wide-awake young branch manager with the brilliant future who got drunk and sick one afternoon and threw up into the hotel swimming pool during the company convention in Florida two years ago wasn't fired, although everyone knew he would not be permitted to remain. He knew it, too. Probably nothing was ever said to him. But he knew it. And four weeks after the convention ended, he found a better job with another company and resigned.

Green, on the other hand, does fire people, at least two or three people every year, and makes no secret of it; in fact, he makes it a point to let everyone know immediately after he *has* fired someone. Often, he will fire someone for no better reason than to cause discussion about himself or

It's always better, and safer, and more effective, to preserve the distinction between executive and subordinate, employer and employee, even in bed. (*Especially* in bed.)

to wake the rest of us up for a while. Most of us who won't ever amount to anything really big here, including Green, do tend to sink into lethargy and coast along sluggishly on the energy and new ideas that helped us make it safely through the year before. That's one of the reasons we won't ever amount to anything much. Most of the men who do make it toward the top are persistent hard workers if they are nothing else (and they are frequently nothing else. Ha, ha).

Sometimes the people Green fires are people he likes personally whose work is good enough (that may, in fact, be just the reason he does fire them—that he has no reason). Then he will grow compassionate and become seriously concerned with their plight (as though he were not the one who created it). He will begin an earnest effort to find other jobs for them somewhere else in the company. He is usually not successful, for his zest for catty advantage quickly replaces his original (and uncharacteristic) good intention, and his approach turns malicious and self-defeating.

'He'd be perfect for you,' is one method Green likes to use in recommending someone in his department to someone who is the head of another department. 'He just isn't good enough for me.'

Once he has made this point in enough places, he soon forgets about the people he has fired, and they go away.

He is charming (ha, ha). At the important company planning sessions that are held out of town every three months at some luxurious resort hotel or plush country club with a well-known golf course, division and department heads (I am told) normally do not argue or complain or express dissatisfaction aloud with each other's work or viewpoint. But Green does: Green criticizes, ridicules, and disparages impatiently, and he always protests vehemently against any cuts in his own budget or any new curtailments of his activities. Then he is sorry. Green rocks the boat impetuously, and is fearful afterward that he is going to sink. He is better read than most people in the company and affects a suave, intellectual superiority that makes even Arthur Baron slightly uncomfortable and makes Andy Kagle and everyone else in the Sales Department feel crude and graceless. (I am much better educated than Green is and, I think, more intelligent, but he is glib and forward, and I am not.) News of Green's repartee and audacious bad behavior at these planning sessions (Green does not even play golf) usually trickles down to us (mainly through Green himself) and we are often proud to be working for him; but I know he is tormented each time by the fear that this time he has at last gone too far. Green worries that none of the important people in the company really like him, and he's right; he is wrong, though, when he surmises it is only because they envy him. (He really isn't likable.) And then there are the many other worries that I know assail Green because the company is large and mainly Protestant.

Green, for example, is afraid of Phillip Reeves, a timid, underpaid young employee in Green's own department, and this amuses me greatly because I know that Phillip Reeves, who is Protestant, English, and went to Yale, is afraid of Green; each complains to me about the other. Reeves confides in me because he thinks I am capable, honest, and unpretentious; he knows I drink and lie and whore around a lot, and he therefore feels he can trust me.

'I'm absolutely terrified every time I have to go into his office,' Reeves complains to me about Green. 'He'll make some sarcastic remark as soon as I walk in, and I won't be able to think of a single intelligent thing to say in reply. I freeze. It's as though I'm paralyzed and struck dumb. It's all I can do to nod or shake my head or mumble answers to his questions, and I stand there almost speechless with an idiotic smile on my face while he goes on and on making caustic remarks. I can't say that I blame him. Afterwards I hate myself for being so stupid and tongue-tied.'

'I'm absolutely terrified every time I have to speak to him in my office,' Green complains to me about Phillip Reeves. 'It's those good manners of his, I guess, and that vulgar good breeding. I can cope with good manners and I can cope with good breeding, but I can't cope with good manners *and* good breeding. They throw me off stride, and it's like listening to some total, idiotic stranger running off at the mouth as I hear what I'm saying and realize what I'm doing. I'll make some innocent joke to him when he walks in, just to try to put us both at ease, and he'll just draw to a stop and stare back at me with that icy, superior smile frozen on his face. I can't get a response out of him. I become so rattled that I begin making one asinine remark after another in an effort to be friendly, but he just stands there in supercilious contempt and waits for me to finish. He must despise me by now, and I can't say that I blame him. God knows he does nothing to put *me* at ease, I can tell you that. Afterwards, I hate myself for being so stupid and weak. I wonder why I don't fire him. Because it would be an admission of defeat, that's why, even though his work *is* lousy.'

I do not tell either of them about the other (although I do try to cheer Reeves up). Neither would believe me, and it would do no good. They've got the whammy on each other—it's as plain as that—and nothing can change the whammy that springs up between one person and another and usually lasts a lifetime.

Green's got the whammy on me.

'I think they've decided to fire *me*,' Green blurts out to me unexpectedly. 'Kagle's the one they should get rid of, but I think that he and Horace White have finally persuaded them. Your pal. You hear things. Go find out from Kagle or Brown or someone else just what's going on. Or I'll fire *you*.'

I don't think Green really intends to fire me (but I'm never that confident about it for very long. I'm not secure about it at all on days when I know he is in a bad mood and I see his door shut for long periods of time). I know Green likes me, although we are not close, and confides in me, and I know he likes my work and the way I run my department for him. And I know Green is afraid of Andy Kagle, who likes me also and might try to protect me, and of Arthur Baron, who also likes me (I think he likes me: Arthur Baron always treats everybody as though he likes them—him—even people I know he doesn't like, so how can one be sure?) and might not let Green fire me. Kagle has sworn, in fact, that he *would* protect me if Green ever decides he does want to get rid of me, and that he would take me right into his own department at a much higher salary, just to spite Green, so I seem to be perfectly safe, until I go to Kagle to find out what I can about Green and hear him say, as soon as I walk into his office:

'I think they've finally decided to fire me!'

AND WHERE WOULD I be if that happened?

Andy Kagle, as head of our Sales Department, has a very powerful position with the company and is now afraid of losing it.

He may be right. His name is all wrong. (Half wrong. Andrew is all right, but Kagle?) So are his clothes. He shows poor judgment in colors and styles, as well as in fabrics, and his suits and coats and shirts do not fit him well enough. He moves to madras and paisley months after others have gone to linen or hopsack or returned to worsted and seersucker. He wears terrible brown shoes with *fleur-de-lis* perforations. He wears anklets (and I want to scream or kick him when I see his shin). Kagle is a stocky man of less than middle height and was born with a malformation of the hip and leg (which also doesn't help his image much); he walks with a slight limp.

Kagle has ability and experience, but they don't count anymore. What does count is that he has no tone. His manners are not good. He lacks wit (his wisecracks are bad, and so are the jokes he tells) and did not go to college, and he does not mix smoothly enough with people who did go to college. He knows he is awkward. He is not a hearty extrovert; he is a nervous extrovert, the worst kind (especially to other nervous extroverts), and so he may be doomed.

Kagle is one of those poor fellows who started at the bottom and worked his way up, and it shows. He is a self-made man and unable to hide it. He knows he doesn't fit, but he doesn't know when he doesn't or why, or how to alter himself so that he will fit in as well as he should. Gauche is what he is, and gauche is what he knows he is (although he is so gauche he doesn't even know what the word *gauche* means, but Green does, and so do I). He has a good record as head of sales, but that hardly matters. (Nothing damages us much anymore.) He thinks it counts. He really thinks that what he does is more important than what he is, but I know he's wrong and that the beautiful Countess Consuelo Crespi (if there is such a thing) will always matter more than Albert Einstein, Madame Curie, Thomas Alva Edison, Andy Kagle, and me.

Kagle is a church-going Lutheran with a strong anti-Catholic bias that he confides to me in smirking, bitter undertones when we are alone. He begins small meetings at which Catholic salesmen are present with joking references to the Pope in an effort to radiate an attitude of camaraderie. The jokes are bad, and nobody laughs. I have advised him to stop. He says he will. He doesn't. He seems compelled.

Kagle is not comfortable with people on his own level or higher. He tends to sweat on his forehead and upper lip, and to bubble in the corners of his mouth. He feels he doesn't belong with them. He is not much at ease with people who work for him. He tries to pass himself off as one of them. This is a gross (and gauche) mistake, for his salesmen and branch managers don't want him to identify with them. To them, he is management; and they know that they are nearly wholly at his mercy, with the exception of the several salesmen below him from very good families above him who do mingle smoothly with higher executives in the company who have *him* at *their* mercy, making him feel trapped and squeezed in between.

Kagle relies on Johnny Brown, whom he fears and distrusts, to keep the salesmen in line (to be the bad guy for him). And Brown does this job efficiently and with great relish. (Brown is related to Black, by his marriage to Black's niece.) Brown's success in scaring the salesmen merely strengthens Kagle's insecurity and weakens his sense of control. Kagle is convinced that Brown is after his job, but he lacks the courage to confront Brown, transfer him, or fire him. Kagle (wisely) avoids a showdown with Brown, who is blunt and belligerent with almost everybody, especially in the afternoon if he's been drinking at lunch. Kagle would rather go out of town on an unnecessary business trip than have a showdown here with anybody about anything, and he usually manufactures excuses for travel whenever his problems here or at home with his wife and children build toward a crisis he wants other people to settle. He hopes they'll be over by the time he returns, and they usually are.

With the exception of Brown (whom Kagle hates, fears, and distrusts, and can do nothing about), Kagle tries to like everyone who works for him and to have everyone like him. He is reluctant to discipline his salesmen or reprimand them, even when he (or Brown) catches them cheating on their expense accounts or lying about their sales calls or business trips. (Kagle lies about his own business trips and, like the rest of us, probably cheats at least a little on his expense accounts.) He is unwilling to get rid of people, even those who turn drunkard, like Red Parker, or useless in other ways. This is one of the criticisms heard about him frequently. (It is occasionally made against him by the same people other people want him to get rid of.) He won't, for example, retire Ed Phelps, who wants to hang on. ('I'd throw half those lying sons of bitches right out on their ass,' Brown enjoys bragging out loud to me and Kagle about Kagle's sales force, as though challenging

Kagle to do the same. 'And I'd put the other half of those lazy bastards on notice.')

Kagle wants desperately to be popular with all the 'lying sons of bitches' and 'lazy bastards' who work for him, even the clerks, receptionists, and typists, and goes out of his way to make conversation with them; as a result, they despise him. The more they despise him, the better he tries to be to them; the better he is to them, the more they despise him. There are days when his despair is so heavy that he seems almost incapable of stirring from his office or allowing anyone (but me) in to see him. He keeps his door shut for long periods of time, skips lunch entirely rather than allow even his secretary to deliver it, and does everything he can by telephone.

Kagle is comfortable with me (even on his very bad days), and I am comfortable with him. Sometimes he sends for me just to have me confirm or deny rumors he has heard (or made up) and help dispel his anxieties and shame. I do not test or threaten him; I pose no problem; on the contrary, he knows I aid him (or try to) in handling the problems created by others. Kagle trusts me and knows he is safe with me. Kagle doesn't scare me any longer. (In fact, I feel that I could scare him whenever I chose to, that he is weak in relation to me and that I am strong in relation to him, and I have this hideous urge every now and then while he is confiding in me to shock him suddenly and send him reeling forever with some brutal, unexpected insult, or to kick his crippled leg. It's a weird mixture of injured rage and cruel loathing that starts to rise within me and has to be suppressed, and I don't know where it comes from or how long I will be able to master it.) Kagle has lost faith in himself; this could be damaging, for people here, like people everywhere, have little pity for failures, and no affection.

I have pity for Kagle (as though I have already delivered my insult or kicked him in his deformed leg viciously—I know it will happen sooner or later, the wish is sometimes so strong), as I have pity for myself. I am sorry for him because he is basically a decent person, if not especially dazzling or admirable. I do worry and sympathize with him often, because he has been good to me from the day I came to work here for Green, and is good to me still. He makes my job easier. He relies on my judgment, takes my word, and backs me up in disputes I have with his salesmen. Many of his salesmen, particularly the new ones, hold me in some kind of awe because they sense I operate under his protection. (A number of the old ones who are not doing well hold me to blame, I'm sure, for having helped bring them to ruin.) Invariably in these disagreements with his salesmen, I am right and they are wrong. I am patient, practical, rational, while they are emotional and insistent. It is easy for me to be practical and rational in these situations because I am not the least bit endangered by the business problems that threaten *them*.

Kagle often comments jokingly to Arthur Baron and other important people, sometimes even in my presence, that I would be much better in Green's job than Green is;

Kagle does this with a gleam of mischief if I am there, because I have begged him not to. I am not certain if Kagle really believes I would be better than Green or is merely making an amiable gesture that he thinks will honor me and get back to Green to irritate and concern him. Because Andy Kagle is good to me and doesn't scare me any longer, I despise him a little bit too.

I TRY MY best to conceal it (although I am often surprised to discover a harder edge to my sarcasms and admonitions than I intended. There is something cankered and terrifying inside me that wishes to burst out and demolish him, lame and imperfect as he is). I try my best to help and protect him in just about every way I can. I am the one who even offers regularly to carry censures and instructions from him to Johnny Brown that he shrinks from delivering himself, although I will never risk anything with Brown after lunch if I can possibly avoid it. Along with everyone else who knows Brown, I endeavor to steer clear of him after lunch (unless I need him on my side in an argument with someone else), when he is apt to be red-eyed and irritable with drink and in a contrary, bellicose mood. Brown in a bad temper with whiskey working inside him always gives the clear impression that he is eager for a fist fight. And there is no doubt that with his deep chest, sturdy shoulders, and thick, powerful hands, he can handle himself in one. And there is also no doubt that Brown is usually right.

The current (and recurrent) antagonism between Kagle and Brown is over call reports again. The salesmen are reluctant to fill out these small printed pink, blue, and white forms (pink for prospects, blue for active, and white for formerly active; that is, accounts that have lapsed and are therefore prospects again, though not necessarily lively ones) describing with some hope and detail the sales calls they have made (or allege they have made). The salesmen are reluctant to come to grips with any kind of paperwork more elaborate than writing out order forms; they especially hate to fill out their expense account reports and fall weeks, sometimes months, behind. The salesmen know beforehand that most of the information they will have to supply in their call reports will be false. Brown maintains that call reports are a waste of everybody's time, and he is reluctant to compel the salesmen to fill them out. Kagle is afraid of Brown, and he is reluctant to compel Brown to compel the salesmen to fill them out.

But Arthur Baron wants the call reports. Arthur Baron has no other way of keeping familiar with what the salesmen are up to (or say they are) and a no more reliable source of knowledge on which to base his own decisions and reports, even though he is certainly aware that most of the knowledge on which he bases his decisions and prepares his own reports is composed of lies.

I try to keep out of it and expel an air of innocence and sympathetic understanding to all concerned. I would rather sit here in my office writing, doodling, flirting on the

telephone with Jane, or talking to a good girl named Penny
I've known a long time, or classifying people in the company and constructing my Happiness Charts, than get
mixed up in this one. I don't care about the call reports and
don't have to. The matter is trivial; yet, it seems to be one
of those trivial matters that might destroy a person or
two, and I don't see how I can gain favor with one person
in this situation without losing favor with another. So, pru-
dently, I contrive to keep as far away from it as I can,
although I *will* manage to mention every now and then to
a salesman I happen to be with on some other business
that Kagle, Brown, or Arthur Baron has been asking about
his call reports and that it is extremely urgent they be
handed in as soon as possible for prompt study and evalu-
ation. (I don't manage to mention—and never would—that
I think they're a waste of everybody's time but mine.)

In this and other small ways I do what I can to be of help
to Kagle (and Brown) (and Arthur Baron). I give him advice
and I bring him gossip and news and portents from other
parts of the company that I think will be of value or concern
to him.

'What do you hear?' he wants to know.

'About what?'

'You know.'

'What do you mean?'

'Jesus Christ,' he complains, 'you used to be truthful
with me. Now I can't even trust you, either.'

'What are you talking about?'

'I hear that I'm out and Brown's in, and that you probably know all about it. I was tipped off in Denver.'

'You're full of shit.'

'I like your honesty.'

'I like yours.'

Kagle grins mechanically, sardonically, and moves with his slight limp across the carpet of his office to close the door. I smile back at him and settle smugly into his brown leather armchair. I always feel very secure and very superior when I'm sitting inside someone's office with the door closed and other people, perhaps Kagle or Green or Brown, are doing all the worrying on the outside about what's going on inside. Kagle has a large, lush corner office in which he seems out of place. He looks nervous and tries to smile as he comes back and sits down behind his desk.

'Seriously, you hear everything,' he says to me. 'Haven't you heard anything?'

'About what?'

'About me.'

'No.'

'The grapevine says I'm finished. They're going to listen to Green and Horace White and get rid of me. Brown's got the job.'

'Who told you that?'

'I can't name names. But I was tipped off by people in Denver who passed it along to me in strictest confidence. It's true. You can take my word for it.'

'You're full of shit again.'

'No, I'm not.'

'There's nobody in our Denver office who would know something like that or tip you off about it if they did.'

'Only about the Denver part. The rest is true.'

'You tell terrible lies,' I say. 'You tell the worst lies of anybody in the whole business. I don't see how you ever made it as a salesman.'

Kagle grins for an instant to acknowledge my humor and then turns glum again.

'Brown tells you things,' he says. 'Hasn't he given any hints?'

'No.' I shake my head. (Everybody seems to think I know everything. 'You know everything,' Brown said to me. 'What's going on?' 'I didn't even know there was anything going on,' I answered. Jane asked: 'What's going on? Are they really getting rid of the whole Art Department?' 'I wouldn't *let* them get rid of you, honey,' I answered. 'Even if I had to pay your salary myself.')

I shake my head again. 'And it's probably not true. They'd never put Brown in. He fights with everybody.'

'Then you *have* heard something,' Kagle exclaims.

'No, I haven't.'

'Who would they put in?'

'Nobody. Andy, why don't you stop all this horseshit and buckle down to your job if you're so really worried? If you're really so worried, why don't you start doing the things you're supposed to do?'

'What am I supposed to do?'

'The things you're supposed to do. Stop trying to be such a good guy to all the people who work for you. You ain't succeeding, and nobody wants you to be. You're a member of management now. Your sales force is your enemy, not your buddy, and you're supposed to be theirs and drive them like slaves. Brown is right.'

'I don't like Brown.'

'He knows his business. Make Ed Phelps retire.'

'No.'

'That's what Horace White wants you to do.'

'Phelps is an old man now. He wants to stay.'

'That's why you have to force him out.'

'His son was divorced last year. His daughter-in-law just took his granddaughter away to Seattle. He might never see the little girl again.'

'That's all very sad.'

'How much does it cost the company to keep him on, even if he doesn't do anything?'

'Very little.'

'Then why should I make him retire?'

(Kagle is right, here, and I like him enormously for his determination to let Phelps stay. Phelps is old and will soon be dead, anyway, or too sick to continue.)

'Because he's past the official retirement age. And Horace White wants you to.'

'I don't like Horace White,' Kagle observes softly, irrelevantly. 'And he doesn't like me.'

'He knows his business also,' I point out.

'How can I tell it to Ed Phelps?' Kagle wants to know. 'What could I say to him? Will you do it for me? It's not so easy, is it?'

'Get Brown to do it,' I suggest.

'No.'

'It's part of *your* job, not mine.'

'But it's not so easy, is it?'

'That's why they pay you so much.'

'I don't get so much,' he digresses almost automatically, 'what with taxes and all.'

'Yes, you do. And stop traveling all the time. Nobody likes that. What the hell were you doing in Denver all this week when there's nothing going on there and you're supposed to be here organizing the next convention and working on your sales projections?'

'I've got Ed Phelps working on the convention.'

'A lot he'll do.'

'And my sales projections are always wrong.'

'So what? At least they're done.'

'What else?'

'Play more golf. Talk to Red Parker and buy a blue blazer. Buy better suits. Wear a jacket in the office and keep your shirt collar buttoned and your necktie up tight around your neck where it belongs. Jesus, look at you right now. You're supposed to be a distinguished white-collar executive.'

'Don't take the name of the Lord in vain,' he jokes.

'Don't you.'

'I've got a good sales record,' he argues.

'Have you got a good sports jacket?' I demand.

'Jesus Christ, what does a good sports jacket matter?'

'More than your good sales record. Nobody wears jackets with round leather patches on the elbows to the office, unless it's on a weekend. Get black shoes for your blue and gray suits. And stop driving into the city in your station wagon.'

'Okay,' he gives in with a gloomy, chastised smile and exhales a long, low whistle of mock surprise and resignation. 'You win.' He gets up slowly and moves toward the coat rack in the corner of his office for his jacket. 'I promise. I'll get a blue blazer.'

It will be too big—I can see it in advance—and hang over his shoulders and sag sloppily around his chest, and he will probably get his worsted blue blazer just about the time the rest of us have switched to mohair or shantung or back to madras, plaids, and seersucker. It is already too late for him, I suspect; I suspect it is no longer in his power (if it ever was in his power) to change himself to everyone's satisfaction. For the moment, though (while I am still with him), he makes an effort: he buttons his shirt collar, and slides tight to his neck the knot of his tie, and puts on his jacket. It is a terrible jacket of coarse, imitation tweed, with oval suede patches at the elbows.

'Better?' he wants to know.

'Not much.'

'I'll throw out these brown shoes.'

'That will help.'

It is already too late for him, I suspect; I suspect it is no longer in his power (if it ever was in his power) to change himself to everyone's satisfaction

'How's Green treating you these days?' he asks casually.

'Pretty good,' I reply. 'Why?'

'If you were in my department,' he offers with a cagey, more confident air, and the beginnings of a mischievous smile, 'I would let you make as many speeches as you want to at the next convention. The salesmen are always very interested in the work you're doing for them and what you have to say.'

'So long,' I answer. 'I'll see you around.'

We both laugh, because we each know what the other wants and where the fears and sore spots are. Kagle knows I want to keep my job and be allowed to make a speech at the next company convention. (God dammit—it would be an honor and an act of recognition, even if it is only three minutes, and I've earned it and I want it, and that's all!) And I know that Kagle wants my help in defending himself against Green (and Brown) (and Black) (and White) (and Arthur Baron, as well).

'You'll let me know if you do hear anything, won't you?' he asks, as we walk to the door.

'Of course I will,' I assure him.

'But don't ask questions,' he cautions with a dark, moody snicker. 'You might give them the idea.'

We laugh.

AND WE ARE both still chuckling when Kagle opens the door of his office and we find my secretary outside talking to his secretary.

'Oh, Mr Slocum,' she sings out cheerily, because that is her way, and I wish I were rid of her. 'Mr Baron wants to see you right away.'

Kagle pulls me to the side. 'What does he want?' he asks with alarm.

'How should I know?'

'Go see him.'

'What did you think I was going to do?'

'And come and tell me if he says anything about getting rid of me.'

'Sure.'

'You will, won't you?'

'Of course I will. For Christ sakes, Andy, can't you trust me?'

'Where are *you* going?' Green wants to know, as I pass him in the corridor on my way to Arthur Baron's office.

'Arthur Baron wants to see me.'

Green skids to a stop with a horrified glare; and it's all I can do not to laugh in his face.

'What does he want with *you*?' Green wants to know.

'I haven't any idea.'

'You'd better go see him.'

'I thought of doing that.'

'Don't be so God-damned sarcastic,' Green snaps back at me angrily, and I lower my eyes, abashed and humbled by his vehemence. 'I'm not even sure I trust *you*, either.'

'I'm sorry, Jack,' I mumble. 'I didn't intend that to sound rude.'

'You come see me as soon as you've finished talking to him,' he orders. 'I want to know what he says. I want to know if I'm being fired or not.'

'What was Kagle talking to you about?' Brown asks when I bump into him.

'He wanted to know what you were up to while he was away in Denver.'

'I was correcting his mistakes and protecting his God-damned job, that was what I was up to,' Brown retorts.

'That's just what I told him.'

'You're a liar,' Brown tells me pleasantly.

'Johnny, that's what they pay me for.'

'But everybody knows it . . .'

'So?'

' . . . so I guess it doesn't matter.'

'A diplomat, Johnny. Not a liar.'

'Yeah, a diplomat,' Brown agrees with a gruff and hearty laugh. 'You lying son of a bitch.'

'I was just coming to see you,' Jane says to me. 'I want to show you this layout.'

I stare brazenly at her tits. 'I can see your layout.' She starts to giggle and blush deliciously, but I turn serious. 'Not now, Jane. I have to go see Arthur Baron.'

'Oh, hello, Mr Slocum,' Arthur Baron's secretary says to me. 'How are you?'

'You look fine today.'

The door to Arthur Baron's office is closed, and I don't know how to cope with it, whether to turn the knob and go right in or knock diffidently and wait to be asked. But Arthur Baron's twenty-eight-year-old secretary, who is fond of me and having trouble with her husband (he's probably queer), nods encouragingly and motions me to go right through. I turn the knob gingerly and open the door. Arthur Baron sits alone at his desk and greets me with a smile. He rises and comes forward slowly to shake my hand. He is always very cordial to me (and everyone) and always very gentle and considerate. Yet I am always afraid of him. He's got the whammy on me, I guess (just as everyone I've ever worked for in my whole life has had the whammy on me), and I guess he always will.

'Hello, Bob,' he says.

'Hi, Art.'

'Come in.' He closes the door noiselessly.

'Sure.'

'How are you, Bob?'

'Fine, Art. You?'

'I want you to begin preparing yourself,' he tells me, 'to replace Andy Kagle.'

'KAGLE?' I ASK.

'Yes.'

'Not Green?'

'No.' Arthur Baron smiles, knowledgeable and reassuring. 'We don't really think you're ready for Green's job yet.'

There is polite irony here, for we both know that Kagle's job is bigger and more important than Green's, and that

Green would be subordinate to Kagle if Kagle were of stronger character. The proposition stuns me, and for a few bewildered seconds I have absolutely no idea what to say or do or what expression to keep on my face. Arthur Baron watches me steadily and waits.

'I've never done any real selling,' I say finally, very meekly.

'We won't want you to do any,' he replies. 'We want you to manage. You're loyal and intelligent and you've got good character and good work habits. You seem to have a good understanding of policy and strategy, and you get along well with all kinds of people. You're diplomatic. You're perceptive and sensitive, and you seem to be a good administrator. Is that enough to encourage you?'

'Kagle's a good man, Art,' I say.

'He's a good salesman, Bob,' Arthur Baron replies, emphasizing the distinction. 'And you'll probably be allowed to keep him on as a salesman if we decide to make the change and you decide you want to.'

'I know I'd want to.'

'We'll probably let you keep him as an assistant even, or as a consultant on special projects with people he'd be good with. But he hasn't been a good manager, and we don't think he's going to be able to get better. Kagle doesn't go along with the rest of us on too many things, and that's very important in his job. He lies a lot. Horace White wants me to get rid of him just because he does tell lies to us. He still travels too much, although I've told him I want him to spend more time here. He dresses terribly. He still wears brown shoes. That shouldn't count, I know, but it does count, and he ought to know that by now. He doesn't send in my call reports.'

'Most of the stuff on the call reports isn't true.'

'I know that. But I have to have them anyway for my own work.'

'Brown is in charge of that,' I have to point out.

'He doesn't control Brown.'

'That isn't easy.'

'He's afraid of him.'

'So am I,' I admit.

'And so am I,' he admits. 'But I would control him or get rid of him if he worked for me. Would you?'

'Brown is married to Black's niece.'

'I wouldn't let that matter. We wouldn't let Black interfere if it came to doing something about Brown.'

'Would you let me fire him?'

'If you decided you really wanted to, although we'd prefer to transfer him. Kagle could have had him fired, but by now Brown has a better grasp of specifics than he has. Kagle never wants to fire anybody, even the ones who are drunks or dishonest or useless in other ways. He won't fire Parker or retire Phelps, and he doesn't cooperate with Green. And he still discriminates in the people he hires, although he's been warned about that, too.'

'It's a very big job,' I say.

'We think you might be able to handle it.'

'If I couldn't?'

'Let's not think about that now.'

'I have to,' I say with a grin.

He grins back sympathetically. 'We'd find another good job for you somewhere else in the company if you found you wanted to stay here, unless you did something disgraceful or dishonest, and I'm sure that wouldn't happen. You don't have to decide now. This is just an idea of mine, and it's anything but definite, so please keep it secret. But we are trying to look ahead, and we'd like to know what we're going to do by convention time. So give it some serious thought, will you, and let me know if you would take it if we did decide to move Kagle out and give it to you. You don't have to take it if you don't want to—I promise you that—and you won't be penalized if you don't.' He smiles again as he stands up and continues in a lighter tone. 'You'll still get your raise this year and a good cash bonus. But we think you should. And you might just as well begin preparing yourself while you make up your mind.'

'What should I do?'

'Keep close to Kagle and the salesmen and try to find out even more about everything that's happening. Decide what realistic goals to establish and what changes you would have to make to achieve them if we did put you in charge.'

'I like Andy Kagle.'

'So do I.'

'He's been very good to me.'

'It isn't your fault. We'd move him out anyway. He'll probably be happier working for you on special projects. Will you think about it?'

'Of course.'

'Good. You'll keep this quiet, won't you?'

'Sure.'

'Thank you, Bob.'

'Thank you, Art.'

'WHAT DID ARTHUR BARON want?' Green demands, the instant I'm out in the corridor.

'Nothing,' I answer.

'Did he say anything?'

'No.'

'Anything about me, I mean.'

'No.'

'Well, what did he say? He must have wanted to see you about something.'

'He wants me to put some jokes in a speech his son has to make at school.'

'Is that all?' Green snorts with contempt, satisfied. 'I could do that,' he sneers. 'Better than you.'

Up yours, I think in reply, because I know I could squash him to the ground and make him crawl like a caterpillar if I ever do find myself in Kagle's job. But he does believe me, doesn't he?

'What did Arthur Baron want?' Johnny Brown asks.

'He wants me to put some jokes in a speech his son has to make at school.'

'You're still a liar.'

'A diplomat, Johnny.'

'But I'll find out.'

'Should I start looking for another job?' asks Jane.

'I've got a job you can do, right here at hand.'

'You're terrible, Mr Slocum,' she laughs, her color rising with embarrassment and pleasure. She is aglow, tempting. 'You're worse than a boy.'

'I'm better than a boy. Come into my office now and I'll show you. What boy that you go with has an office with a couch like mine and pills in the file cabinet?'

'I'd like to,' she says (and for a second I am in terror that she will). 'But Mr Kagle is waiting for you there.'

'What did Arthur Baron want?' Kagle asks as soon as I step inside my office and find him lurking anxiously in a corner there.

I close the door before I turn to look at him. He is shabby again, and I am dismayed and angry. The collar of his shirt is unbuttoned, and the knot of his tie is inches down. (For a moment, I have an impulse to seize his shirt front furiously in both fists and begin shaking some sense into him; and at exactly the same time, I have another impulse to kick him as hard as I can in the ankle or shin of his crippled leg.) His forehead is wet with beads of perspiration, and his mouth is glossy with a suggestion of spittle, and dry with the powdered white smudge of what was probably an antacid tablet.

'Nothing,' I tell him.

'Didn't he say anything?'

'No. Nothing important.'

'About me?'

'Not a word.'

'You mean that?'

'I swear.'

'Well, I'll be damned,' Kagle marvels with relief. 'What did he talk about? Tell me. He must have wanted to see you about something.'

'He wants me to put some jokes in a speech his son has to make at school.'

'Really?'

'Yeah.'

'And he didn't say anything about me, anything at all?'

'No.'

'Or the call reports or the trip to Denver?'

'No.'

'Ha! In that case, I may be safe, you know. I might even make vice-president this year. What did he talk about?'

'Just his son. And the speech. And the jokes.'

'I'm probably imagining the whole thing,' he exclaims exultantly. 'You know, maybe I can use those same jokes someday if one of *my* kids is ever asked to make a speech at school.' He frowns, his face clouding suddenly with a distant distress. 'Both my kids are no good,' he reminds himself aloud abstractedly. 'Especially the boy.'

Kagle trusts me also. And I'm not so sure I want him to.

'Andy,' I call out to him suddenly. 'Why don't you play it safe? Why don't you behave? Why don't you start doing everything everybody wants you to do?'

He is startled. 'Why?' he cries. 'What's the matter?'

'To keep your job, that's why, if it's not too late. Why don't you start trying to go along? Stop telling lies to Horace White. Don't travel so much. Transfer Parker to another office if you can't get him to stop drinking and retire Ed Phelps.'

'Did somebody say something?'

'No.'

'Then how do you know all that?' he demands. 'Who told you?'

'You did,' I bark back at him with exasperation and disgust. 'You've been telling me about all those things over and over again for months. So why don't you start doing something about them instead of worrying about them all the time and taking chances? Settle down, will you? Control Brown and cooperate with Green, and why don't you hire a Negro and a Jew?'

Kagle scowls grimly and broods in heavy silence for several seconds. I wait, wondering how much is sinking in.

'What would I do with a coon?' he asks finally, as though thinking aloud, his mind wandering.

'I don't know.'

'I could use a Jew.'

'Don't be too sure.'

'We sell to Jews.'

'They might not like it.'

'But what would I do with a coon?'

'You would begin,' I advise, 'by finding something else to call him.'

'Like what?'

'A Black. Call him a Black.'

'That's funny.'

'Yeah.'

'I've always called them coons,' Kagle says. 'I was brought up to call niggers coons.'

'I was brought up to call Negroes coons.'

'What should I do?' he asks. 'Tell me what to do.'

'Grow up, Andy,' I tell him earnestly, trying with all my heart now to help him. 'You're a middle-aged man with two kids and a big job in a pretty big company. There's a lot that's expected of you. It's time to mature. It's time to take it seriously and start doing all the things you should be doing. You know what they are. You keep telling me what they are.'

Kagle nods pensively. His brow furrows as he ponders my advice without any hint of levity. I am getting through to him. I watch him tensely as I wait for his reply. Kagle, you bastard, I want to scream at him desperately as he meditates solemnly, I am trying to help you. Say something wise. For once in your mixed-up life, come to an intelligent conclusion. It's almost as though he hears me, for he makes up his mind finally and his face brightens. He stares up at me with a slight smile and then, while I hang on his words hopefully, says:

'Let's go get laid.'

———

THE COMPANY HAS a policy about getting laid. It's okay.

And everybody seems to know that (although it's not spelled out in any of the personnel manuals). Talking about getting laid is even more okay than doing it, but doing it is okay too, although talking about getting laid with your own wife is never okay. (Imagine: 'Boy, what a crazy bang I got from my wife last night!' That wouldn't be nice, not with gentlemen you associate with in business who might know her.) But getting laid with somebody else's wife is very okay, and so is talking about it, provided the husband is not with the company or somebody anybody knows and likes. The company is in favor of getting laid if it is done with a dash of élan, humor, vulgarity, and skill, without emotion, with girls who are young and pretty or women who are older and foreign or glamorous in some other way, without too much noise and with at least some token gesture toward discretion, and without scandal, notoriety, or any of the other serious complications of romance. Falling in love, for example, is *not* usually okay, although marrying someone else right after a divorce is, and neither is 'having an affair,' at least not for a man.

Getting laid (or talking about getting laid) is an important component of each of the company conventions and a decisive consideration in the selection of a convention site; and the salesmen who succeed in getting laid there soonest are likely to turn out to be the social heroes of the convention, though not necessarily the envy. (That will depend on the quality of whom they find to get laid with.)

Getting laid at conventions is usually done in groups of three or four (two decide to go out and try and take along one or two others). Just about everybody in the company gets laid (or seems to), or at least talks as though he does (or did). In fact, it has become virtually *comme il faut* at company conventions for even the very top and very old, impotent men in the company—in fact, *especially* those—to allude slyly and boastfully to their own and each other's sexual misconduct in their welcoming addresses, acknowledgments, introductions, and informal preambles to speeches on graver subjects. Getting laid is a joking matter on all levels of the company, even with people like Green and Horace White. But it's not a matter for Andy Kagle to joke about now.

'Andy, I'm serious,' I say.

'So,' he says, 'am I.'

I close the door of my office after Kagle leaves, sealing myself inside and shutting everybody else out, and try to decide what to do about my conversation with Arthur Baron. I cancel my lunch appointment and put my feet up on my desk.

I've got bad feet. I've got a jawbone that's deteriorating and someday soon I'm going to have to have all my teeth pulled. It will hurt. I've got an unhappy wife to support and two unhappy children to take care of. (I've got that other child with irremediable brain damage who is neither happy nor unhappy, and I don't know what will happen to him after we're dead.) I've got eight unhappy people working for me who have problems and unhappy dependents of their own. I've got anxiety; I suppress hysteria. I've got politics on my mind, summer race riots, drugs, violence, and teen-age sex. There are perverts and deviates everywhere who might corrupt or strangle any one of my children. I've got crime in my streets. I've got old age to face. My boy, though only nine, is already worried because he does not know what he wants to be when he grows up. My daughter tells lies. I've got the decline of American civilization and the guilt and ineptitude of the whole government of the United States to carry around on these poor shoulders of mine.

And I find I am being groomed for a better job.

And I find—God help me—that I want it.

JOSEPH HELLER WAS one of the twentieth century's best known satirists. He was a pilot with the US Air Corps during the Second World War, and later worked as a copywriter in an advertising agency. His debut novel, *Catch-22*, based on his experiences with the Air Corps, catapulted him to international literary fame and established Heller as a writer capable of voicing the madness of modern life.

Something Happened (from which this book is taken) offers a piercingly sharp satire on suburban and corporate America. Narrated by discontented company executive Bob Slocum, the novel offers a grim portrait of the limits to which we let work push, and ultimately, mould us.

Alongside *Catch-22*, *Something Happened* has been hailed as Joseph Heller's 'other masterpiece'. Heller died in 1999.

RECOMMENDED BOOKS BY JOSEPH HELLER:

Something Happened
Catch-22
God Knows

How to wind down after Work?

Drinking
JOHN CHEEVER

VINTAGE MINIS

Swimming
ROGER DEAKIN

VINTAGE MINIS

Liberty
VIRGINIA WOOLF

VINTAGE MINIS

Death
JULIAN BARNES

VINTAGE MINIS

VINTAGE MINIS

The Vintage Minis bring you the world's greatest writers on the experiences that make us human. These stylish, entertaining little books explore the whole spectrum of life – from birth to death, and everything in between. Which means there's something here for everyone, whatever your story.

vintageminis.co.uk